Innovat

"Self-expression through art is merely a reflection of the soul"
-Lola Mae

"It is only through mastering love of ourselves, that we are able to truly love another"
-Lola Mae

I am donating the proceeds from my book to my son's (Keyonte) education fund. He will be graduating from high school this Spring 2019 and continuing on to college with limited resources. You can also support his college journey by donating to GoFundMe- Keys to Success for Keyonte'.
We appreciate all of your support!

Innovative Expressions

Acknowledgements:
I'd like to give a special thanks to everyone who contributed in helping me create this
Book. It was a journey well worth it! A special thanks goes to my independent publisher, Ashley Nicole Wilkins, who patiently guided and supported me through this process. I'd also like to thank my illustrators for their beautifully created artwork:

Cover by DeShaun Sherrill

Illustrations by:
DeShaun Sherrill, Raquel Rhone, Carlos Marquez, Austin Groebner,
&
Annastocia Cardon

Digitizing by Chrome Digital, San Diego, CA

My illustrators are available for art sales and custom made artwork:

DeShaun Sherrill-
Facebook and Instagram: DSFxArt
Email: DSArt06@yahoo.com

Raquel Rhône-
Facebook: Raquel Rhone
Instagram: raquelsartstudio
Email: Raqueldrhone@gmail.com

Austin Groebner-
Facebook: Austin Groebner
Instagram: aggroebner
Email: aggroebner@gmail.com

Carlos Marquez-
Facebook: Los Reyes

Innovative Expressions

Instagram: ll.los.ll

Annastocia Cardon-
Facebook: Anna Ismee
Instagram: anna_beautiful16
Annastocia is preparing to graduate high school, and she is continuing her education in the medical field with aspirations to obtain her MD/PHD. You can support her educational journey on GoFundMe- Removing The Barriers So Anna Can Succeed.

Innovative Expressions

Copyright © 2019

All rights reserved. No part of this publication may be reproduced, distributed, or transmitted in any form or by any means, including photocopying, recording, or other electronic or mechanical methods, without the prior written permission of the publisher, except in the case of brief quotations embodied in critical reviews and certain other noncommercial uses permitted by copyright law. For permission requests, write to the publisher, addressed "Attention: Permissions Coordinator," at the address below.

Ashley Nicole's Bookshelf

Ordering Information:

Quantity sales. Special discounts are available on quantity purchases by corporations, associations, and others. For details, contact the publisher at the email address below.

Orders by U.S. trade bookstores and wholesalers. Please contact

AuthorAshleyNicole12@gmail.com

Printed in the United States of America

Title of book: Innovative Expressions / Lola Mae

ISBN: 9781095044544

First Edition

Raquel Rhône

Rest In Paradise
Angela Darlene Thomas (Tutt)
January 8, 1957 – September 4, 2008

I am dedicating this book to my biological mother, Angela Darlene Thomas, whom I was
reunited with at age twenty-four. We did not have a lot of time together, as she passed away
one year after we met. In that time she taught me the true meaning of strength, inner healing,
dedication, and perseverance.

My Soul Tie Reconnection

Panic struck by my dream
I jumped up out of my sleep
Face to face with my reality
I was knocking on a quarter century
With no recollection of the goddess that gave birth to me

It was then…I knew we HAD to meet
The years we were kept apart
Began to take a toll on my heart
It was time for our truth to emerge from the dark

Though we didn't coexist
The moment our souls reunited
It was as though they had never been divided
Our realities simply coincided

And through the truth
We were both set free
Our lives were no longer a mystery
Missing each other in misery

Although our time together here was short
It was oh so sweet
You were the missing piece needed to make my puzzle complete

On that night you went to sleep

Who would've ever known your physical presence would become forever obsolete

Losing you was truly a defeat

It left me feeling lost and weak

With my memories of you playing on constant repeat

Because I fear that one day

They'll eventually deplete

I had to ask myself

What is there to gain from this undying pain

As I'd rather celebrate your life

And honor your name

Than allow the question why to drive me insane

Preface

My intention with the collection of my poems in this book is to promote self-love, growth, development, and accountability. I also would like to encourage people of color to embrace the rich culture & spirituality of their ancestors, in hopes of liberating them from the negative systematic programming that's been instilled in people of color. As a poet I have a natural love for the arts, so I decided to accompany my poems with illustrations. I believe all talent deserves to be seen, so I chose to publish more than one artist. A couple of them I've known from childhood, and a few I was blessed to connected with on social media. I hope you all enjoy this collection of poetry and are inspired while gaining a deeper understanding of yourself and others.

TABLE OF CONTENTS

Warrior Goddess- Austin Groebner — Pg. 13

Words Spell Actions Tell- Annastocia Cardon — Pg. 15

Earth Goddess- Raquel Rhone — Pg. 17

We Create- Carlos Marquez — Pg. 19

My One and Only- Annastocia Cardon — Pg. 21

Open Eye- Raquel Rhone — Pg. 23

Nature's Witch- DeShaun Sherrill — Pg. 25

Self Love- Annastocia Cardon — Pg. 28

Twin Flame- Raquel Rhone — Pg. 31

Rise in Love- Carlos Marquez — Pg. 33

Black HIStory- Raquel Rhone — Pg. 36

Zen Men- Austin Groebner — Pg. 38

Wake Up! Rise Up! - Raquel Rhone — Pg. 40

Wombman- DeShaun Sherrill — Pg. 43

About the Author — Pg. 44

Warrior Goddess
Warrior Goddess

A goddess rarely ever cries

And she seldom questions why

This allows her spirit to freely fly

Detached from the physical world

Forgetting to fear and fret

Because in reality there is no death

This is something a goddess learns to accept

So her only focus is to manifest her best

Her higher level of consciousness disconnects her from anything less

Being In tune with spirit and lead by her guides

This is the reason she seldom questions why

A goddess knows she is infinite energy

Which allows her spirit to roam carefree

Forgetting to fear and fret

Because in reality there is no death

Words Spell Actions Tell

Words Spell Actions Tell

Watch their actions

Don't listen to their words

For love is a verb

Not just a four letter word

Their actions will tell

As their words just cast spells

Spelling out intentions shouldn't catch your attention

Most talk is cheap

So don't be weak

And even when using figures of speech

Always remember

It's only their actions that truly do speak

Earth Goddess

Earth Goddess

Earth needs water to mold and shape

Allowing the goddess to procreate

Planting seeds when she's moist and wet

Absorbing energy from all the rest

Learning lessons

Passing tests

Earth needs sun to transmute best

During the night her mind takes flight

Can't help but wonder

What if...and what might

Though the goddess never loses sight

Grounded by gravity

She's unable to escape reality

Is this a victory or a tragedy

We Create

We Create

The law of attraction is like a chemical reaction

Caused by our choice of action and inaction

It ain't God doin' the blessin'

And the devil ain't the one causin' the stressin'

We create

When your conscience is speaking...listen

The choice is yours

To feed your ego

Or feed your divine spirit

Searching for God in all the wrong places

Look within

Tune in

Intuition was given for assistance

So stop the resistance

We create

Free will may be free

But this is not true for the consequences that be

Good or bad

Free will you have

My One and Only

My One and Only

They say you don't know what you have until it's gone

How did I go wrong

His love was oh so strong

He was always there for me

How did I not see

Now I'm left feeling empty

A piece of my heart was taken from me

Left with regret

Trying not to fret

Why'd I put him at second best

When he treated me with the utmost respect

All along I was searching for the one

Not realizing he was my number one

The only one

Always down for me

My one and only

Innovative Expressions

Open Eye

Open Eye

As children of the sun
To be made whole
We must know where we come from

The root of the problem is that we know not our roots
Dug up from the motherland
Replanted in another land
Struggling to prosper and grow on American soil
We can barely bud amongst the hate and turmoil

Yet they make us look superior
By their hidden agenda to make us feel inferior
Which has left us living in fear
Running from unity and our own cultural identity

Our roots are from the motherland of civilization
Yet they say we're uncivilized
Just to justify why they dehumanize

The original hue-man
6 protons 6 neutrons 6 electrons

A carbon melanated being
They labeled a beast
Little do they know
This is stardust they see

Innovative Expressions

Nature's Witch

Nature's Witch

I find it odd that most fear God

I fear karma

Even though it's not her intent to harm ya

She serves what you deserve

And has no mercy for your words

Don't bother to beg and plea

She'll be lookin' like…

Bitch please

Get off your knees

Whether it's in this life or the next

That chick karma never forgets

Calling her a bitch just gets on her wits

Knowing damn well

You created this shit

All she is…

Is nature's witch

What part did you miss

Check how you act

And you won't need to worry what's coming back

Now here are the facts…

Karma doesn't even react

What she really does is match

Match the frequency of your vibration

You control your elevation

Vibrate high

So you won't be constantly wondering why

Looking for answers from the man in the sky

Screaming why me

As you beg & plea

On your knees

While karma's lookin' like…

Bitch please

Self Love

Love

A verb that makes me go hmmmm

It sounds so good

And TV makes it look good

The thought of being in love can be quite entertaining

But reality is...the horror stories keep me questioning and contemplating

They say there are different kinds of love

Love for our family and friends

Love of our interests

As well as that romantic love

And then...

There is self love

Which I see so many people lose

When they quote unquote

Fall in love

Beating...cheating...lying and manipulation

Where does love fit in the equation

How does that work

How can that be

Somebody please...explain this to me

They lost me when they said

Love is pain...love is envious and love is jealous

True authentic love includes protection...happiness and definitely trust

With self love being the greatest love
Watch how they care for themselves
Spiritually...physically and mentally
You'll then know if you want that as your destiny
Never sacrifice self love
For one who knows not how to love

<u>Twin Flame</u>

I pushed you away when I wanted you to stay

All because I couldn't have you my way

I'd tell myself you didn't care

And treat you unfair

When you'd stare

I'd give you that glare

Just to avoid the feelings that were there

Little did I know that stare just said I care

It stemmed from the unconditional love in the air

Even with my empathic trait

I knew I couldn't control your fate

So I put up a gate

Thinking it would keep me safe

Hiding from raw emotion because I couldn't fathom the notion

Wondering how our love potion kept us rockin' in slow motion

It must have been your pure devotion

That I refused to see

Even after my mama told me

I'd constantly question

Why'd he choose me

I come with a fee

My temper tantrums and reckless mouth

Without a doubt

Now I can see

How you were convinced

It was all about me

I hope it's not too late for me to clear my slate

And take control of our cosmic fate

For it is now my turn to reciprocate

My twin flame soul mate

Rise in Love

Do I really want to fall in love

When we fall down

We get hurt

When people fall out

Feelings are hurt

When things fall apart

We feel hurt

Even in the cold autumn breeze

The leaves fall from their trees

So do I really want to fall in love

When we fall for a prank

The joke is on us

I don't want to be pranked by fake love

Or find out it was just lust

I choose to rise in love

I choose to be in love

I choose to prosper in love

Even in the warm spring breeze

The leaves grow and flowers bud

That's nature's way of expressing love

Black HIStory

They gave us a month to celebrate black history

Knowing damn well our truth became a mystery when they rewrote history

And made it HIS- story

HIS- story left out our glory

The greatness from which we came

They want us to see no further than the chains we were put in for their gain

Kidnapped from our kinfolk

Stripped of our language gods and names

Leaving us with generations of pain

And now they have the nerve to call us insane

Though our thoughts were rearranged

While we were in chains

We must now regain

The truth from which we came

No need to feel shame

This is how we beat them at their game

Rest In Peace Victor

Zen Men

A woman must not forget her worth

For her yoniverse is heaven on earth

Life manifests there before birth

Protect your divine feminine energy

As it's not meant to be shared with many

Even though he may see you as a ten

There's a 9.9 chance

That man has yet to find Zen

But trust...

As a goddess you will know when

The moment you meet

You'll be swept off your feet

By his inner state of peace

Wake Up! Rise Up!

Wake Up! Rise Up!

For brighter days we're yearning
But when and how
In circles we keep turning
We're supposed to be evolving
But our minds just keep revolving

Getting smacked in the face when the door stops turning
Smacked by government corruption and the lies being told by mass media production
Smacked by oppression and self-hate
Our reality that they refuse to communicate

We're supposed to be evolving
But our minds just keep revolving

As though we're hamsters spinning on what we want to believe is a freedom wheel
Truth is...this cage was designed for us, not by us, and nothing in it will liberate us
Western philosophy religion and medicine are unnatural to the Eastern Indigenous mind body and soul
But I'm not sure if ya'll hear me though

For brighter days we're yearning
But when and how...

Wake up! Rise up!

Kings and Queens

Return to your noble thrones

Love yourself

Love your people

Embrace your sacred ancestral roots

We are the Alpha and the Omega

Now is the time

Hop off that delusional freedom wheel

And exit the revolving door

So that in chains...you will be no more

Wombman

Wombman

The being in which all human life comes from

Designed and chosen by the creator to port souls into this earthly realm

She is therefore sacred

And the goddess should be treated no less

Her touch is tender like the kiss of the sun

Her voice is soothing like the beat of a drum

Her beauty so intriguing

Her thoughts hold deeper meaning

She is a giver of love

A protector and provider

A nurturer and guider

Stick right beside her

In a wombman's presence you can elevate higher

About the Author

Lola Mae (Lola Martina Medved) was born in St. Paul, MN, on September 10, 1982. At the age of two she was adopted into a Caucasian/biracial home where she was raised in the suburbs. Fitting in and being accepted didn't come easy because her soul has strong ties to its Native American and African roots. She was never quite able to assimilate into a culture she didn't identify with, so she found a home in the few soul tie relationships she developed with those who understood her indigenous nature and spirituality. Writing has been an outlet for Lola Mae since childhood, and she wrote a few poems as a teenager. She was inspired to start writing again a few years ago when her preschool teacher, Pamela Smith, may she Rest in Peace, gifted her a journal when Lola mentioned to her that she would like to write a book. I hope this collective work inspires others to write their first book.

You may also contact Lola Mae via the following:

LolaMae333@yahoo.com

Instagram- @BooksBringSuccess

Facebook- Lola Mae

NOW AVAILABLE ON AMAZON!

Made in the USA
Middletown, DE
05 October 2020